Ladybird

1000 Words and Pictures

compiled by RICHARD POWELL
illustrated by TONY KENYON

All about me

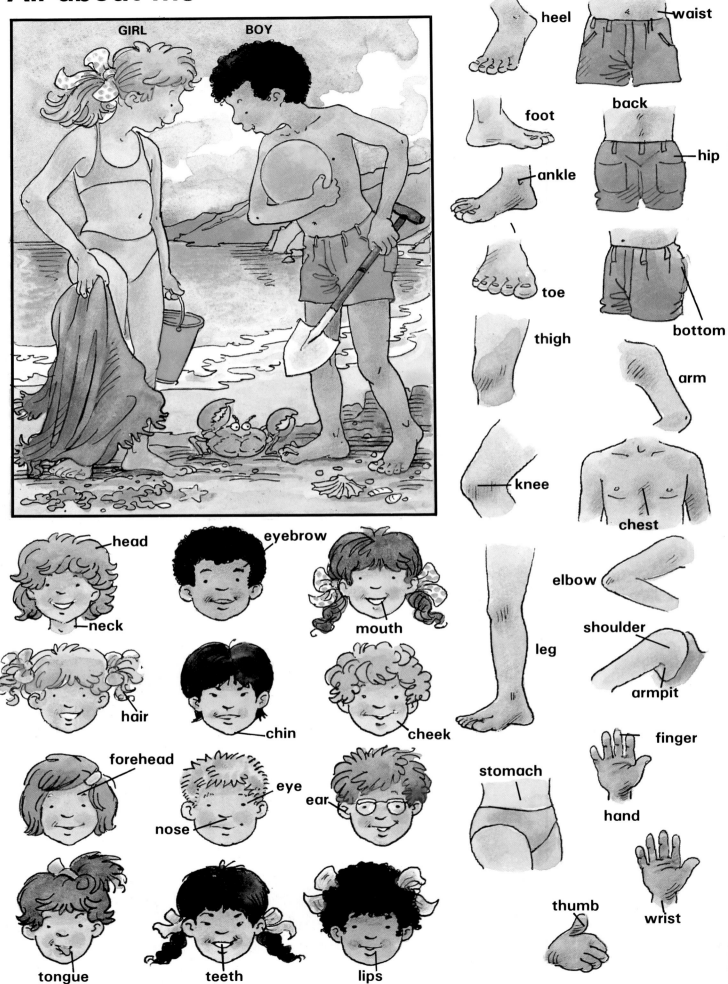

GIRL BOY

heel

waist

foot

back

ankle

hip

toe

bottom

thigh

arm

knee

chest

head

eyebrow

neck

mouth

hair

chin

cheek

elbow

leg

shoulder

armpit

finger

forehead

eye

stomach

ear

nose

hand

tongue

teeth

lips

thumb

wrist

Clothes

sweater

shorts

cardigan

nightdress

shirt

anorak

pants

skirt

pyjamas

tie

vest

tights

scarf

gloves

trousers

T-shirt

handkerchief

socks

dress

blouse

jumper

rainhat

jacket

raincoat

boots

shoes

3

Families

wife/mother/mum

grandad

husband/father/dad

granny

brother/son

sister/daughter

baby

Pets

kennel

kitten

parrot

dog

horse

guinea pig

tortoise

stable

canary

cage

4

grandma
grandpa
aunt
uncle
twins/cousins

hutch
rabbit
puppy
fish
tank
frog
cat
budgerigar
perch
wheel
mouse

5

Homes

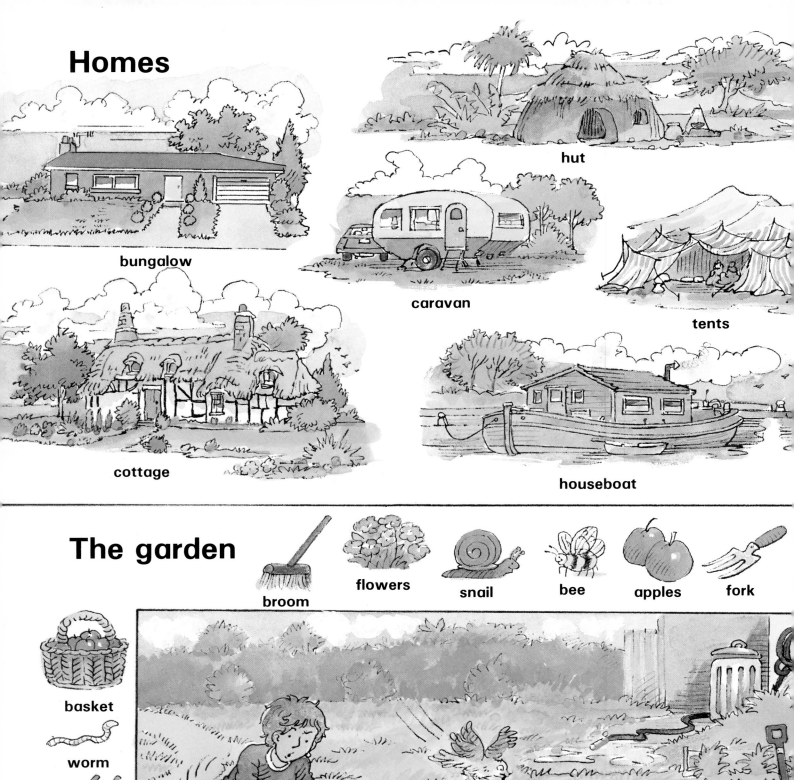

bungalow

hut

caravan

tents

cottage

houseboat

The garden

broom

flowers

snail

bee

apples

fork

basket

worm

ladder

dog

cat

hosepipe

6

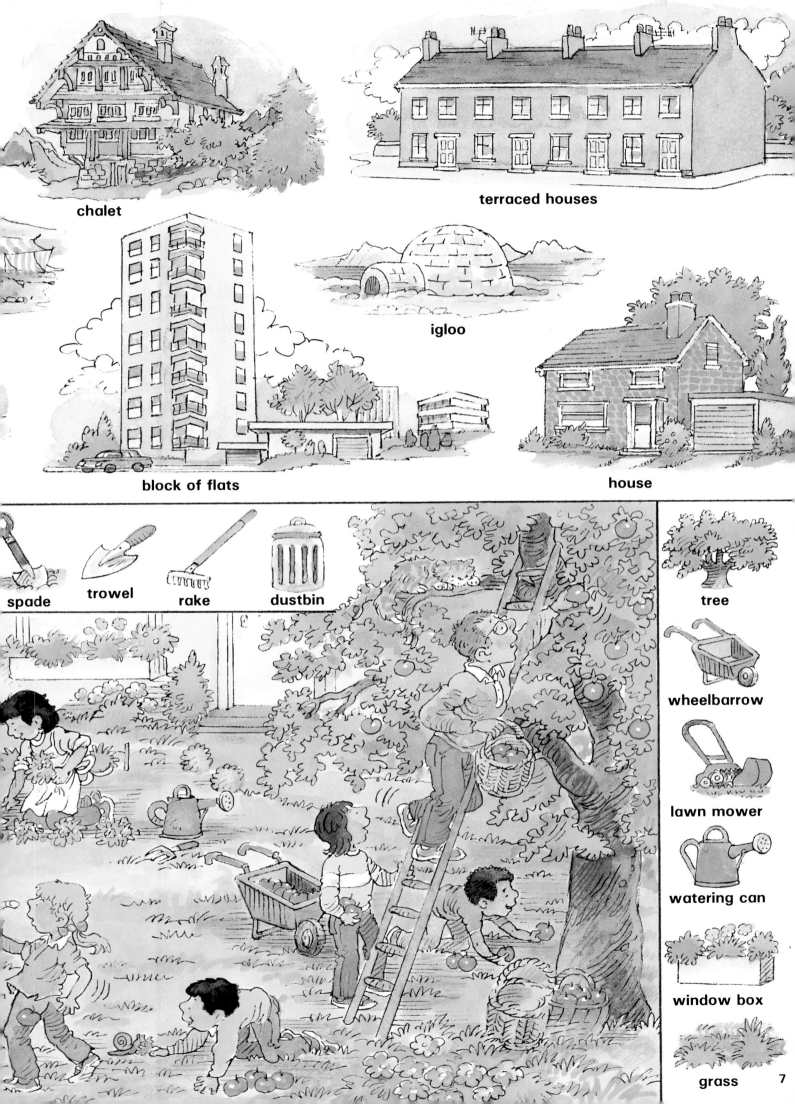

chalet

terraced houses

igloo

block of flats

house

spade

trowel

rake

dustbin

tree

wheelbarrow

lawn mower

watering can

window box

grass

7

The kitchen

tin opener

apron

mop

frying pan

cup

saucer

dog bowl

sink

washing-up liquid

draining board

taps

tea towel

stool

plate

mug

brush

dustpan

iron

cupboard

whisk

washing powder

oven

tray

wooden spoon

pedal bin

kettle

washing machine

sieve

rolling pin

tiles

saucepan

freezer

refrigerator

hob

mixing bowl

ironing board

drawer

9

The living room

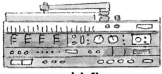
hi-fi

radiator

speaker

table

records

vase

cushion

magazine

rug

clock

picture

armchair

tape

telephone

bookcase

settee

books

lamp

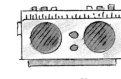
radio

newspaper

television

The dining room

jug

butter dish

spoon

glass

sideboard

tablecloth

salt

pepper

dining chair

curtains

fruit bowl

fork

knife

table mat

bread board

carpet

plant

sauce bottle

plate

wool

door

11

The bedroom

alarm clock

slippers

quilt

toy box

teddy bear

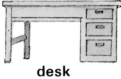
desk

curtains

poster

The bathroom

bubbles

shampoo

towel

mirror

scales

shaver

toilet paper

toilet

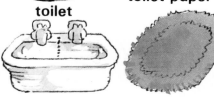
basin

bath mat

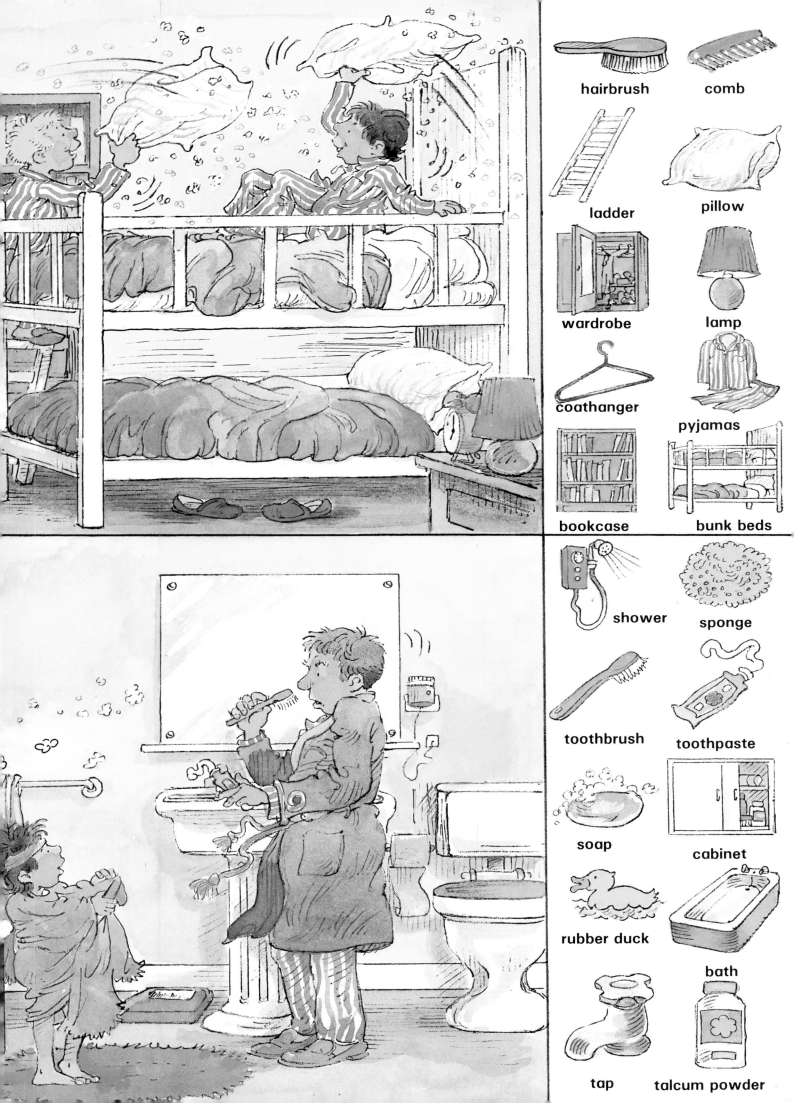

hairbrush

comb

ladder

pillow

wardrobe

lamp

coathanger

pyjamas

bookcase

bunk beds

shower

sponge

toothbrush

toothpaste

soap

cabinet

rubber duck

bath

tap

talcum powder

The street

workman

drain

traffic light

aerial

litter bin

shopping bag

florist shop

lorry

policeman

drill

clock

ice cream van

garage

bicycle

church

bus

bird

baker's shop

van

lamp post

delivery man

pavement

motorcycle

buggy

manhole

driver

car

umbrella

taxi

petrol pump

digger

newsstand

bunch of flowers

water pipe

traffic cone

flats

15

The supermarket

carrots

marrow

cabbage

celery

meat

chicken

cheese

cereal

tins

flour

detergent

yogurt

trolley

milk

jam

basket

toilet rolls

till

bread

fish

eggs

beans
 **tomatoes**
 **cucumbers**
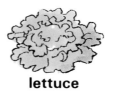 **sweet corn**
lettuce
potatoes
 **melons**

 **onions**

mushrooms

 oranges

 pears

 **apples**

 lemons

 **grapes**

 **pineapple**

 **bananas**

 butter

 margarine

 **sausages**
 **sugar**
 biscuits
 **cashier**
 **juice**
 **cream**
 **customer**

17

In hospital

 plaster cast

 medicine

 bandage

 get well card

 watch

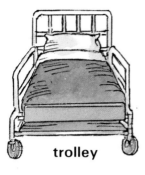 trolley

 stethoscope

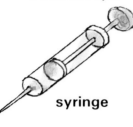 syringe

 nurse

 height chart

 television

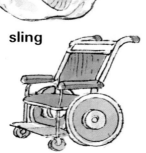 sling

wheelchair

 operating theatre

crutch

doctor

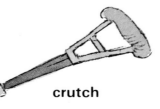 plant

18

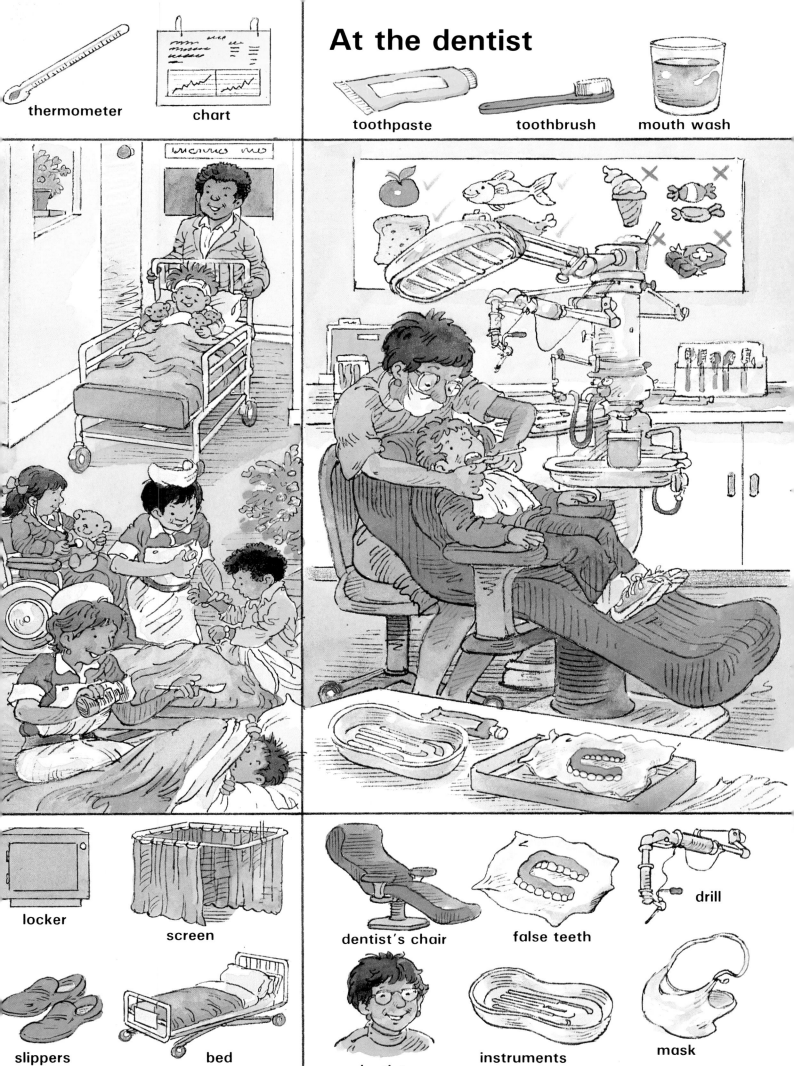

thermometer

chart

At the dentist

toothpaste

toothbrush

mouth wash

locker

screen

slippers

bed

dentist's chair

false teeth

drill

dentist

instruments

mask

The classroom

paper

clock

map

chalk

satchel

glue

ruler

pens

pencils

compass

calendar

bin

scissors

blackboard **books** **crayons** **desk** **paints**

exercise book **rubber** **brush** **jigsaw** **drawing pins** **teacher** **globe**

fish tank **nature chart** **scales** **computer**

21

The park

lead

bone

roller skates

railings

picnic

bench

duck

ribbon

flowers

walking stick

paddling pool

ducklings

slide

cap

swimming costume

litter bin

22

rubber ring

kite

balloon

drinking fountain

swings

bandstand

newspaper

seesaw

grass

skipping rope

flask

roundabout

jogger

pushchair

bicycle

yacht

23

Wild animals and birds

eagle

raccoon

koala

giraffe

beaver

ostrich

panda

gorilla

zebra

leopard

crocodile

flamingo

dolphin

polar bear

hippopotamus

parrot

lion

cubs

kangaroo

rhinoceros

monkey

camel

elephant

pelican

penguin

snake

tiger

bear

seal

walrus

The railway station

mailbag

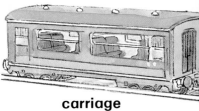

carriage

coal wagon

guard

signal

ticket office

diesel engine

passengers

buffet car

timetable

rucksack

suitcase

cab

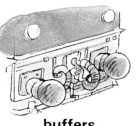

buffers

goods train

driver

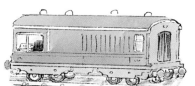

guard's van

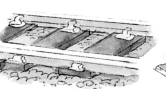

track

luggage trolley

flowers

platform

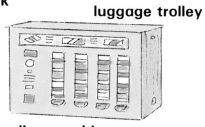

trolley

vending machine

litter bin

The harbour

life jacket

sailing boat

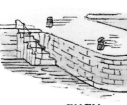

quay

cargo ship

lighthouse

rope

tanker

porthole

seagull

buoy

lobster pot

crane

funnel

mast

fishing net

tug

lifebuoy

anchor

rowing boat

oar

fishing boat

fish

car ferry

flag

scales

fisherman

29

The airport

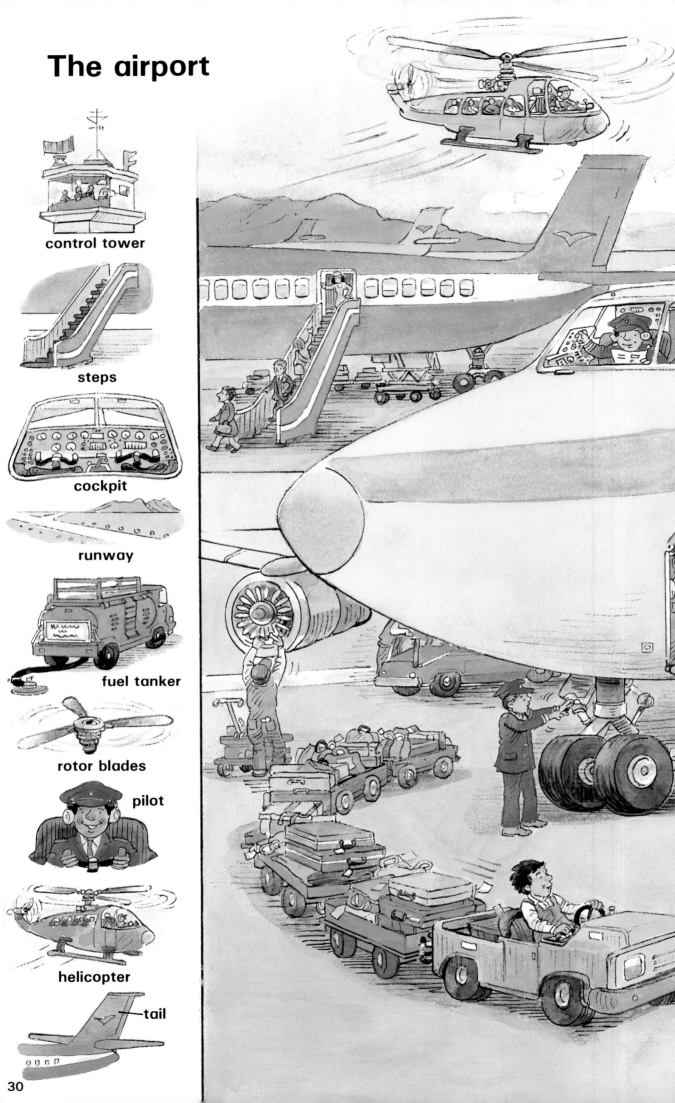

control tower

steps

cockpit

runway

fuel tanker

rotor blades

pilot

helicopter

tail

DANGER
NO
SMOKING

aeroplane

baggage truck

suitcase

hangar

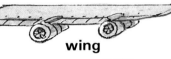

wing

jet engine

landing lights

flight attendant

engineer

windsock

radar

31

The bus station

bus

kiosk

timetable

barrier

queue

bus stop

ticket machine

busker

conductor

flat tyre

snack bar

postcards

parcel

briefcase

shopping bag

driver

33

The building site

drill

wheelbarrow

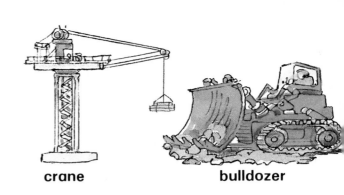
crane   **bulldozer**

electrician   **shovel**

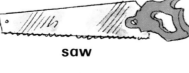
saw

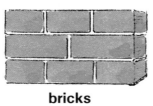
bricks

plumber

ladder

34

trowel

bricklayer

dumper truck

nails

hammer

welder

pick

hard hat

cement

cement mixer

roof tiles

carpenter

scaffolding

35

The garage

spanner

petrol pump

exhaust pipe

pliers

wing mirror

LBL 1

bonnet

boot

seat belt

engine

windscreen

jack

tool box

tyre

steering wheel

bumper

headlight

mechanic

car wash

air pump

fire extinguisher

oil can

litter bin

CP100

On the farm

goose

sheep

lambs

scarecrow

bull

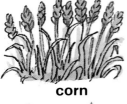
corn

henhouse

plough

baler

combine harvester

farmer

milk tanker

chicks

saddle

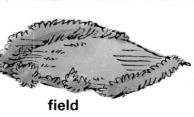
field

stable

silo

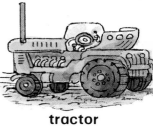
tractor

38

horse

cow

pig

turkey

cockerel

hen

duck

ducklings

sheepdog

straw bales

sack

barn

pond

farmhouse

trailer

hay

gate

pigsty

broom

cart

sickle

cowshed

39

The countryside

leaf

tree

lake

bee

kite

fly

dragonfly

footpath

hiker

ladybird

beetle

rucksack

butterfly

rowing boat

village

field

bridge

river

angler

caravan

squirrel

signpost

fish

otter

fishing rod

nest

rabbit

frog

mountain

waterfall

bush

caterpillar

bird

log

mallet

deer

map

cable car

skier

tent

barbecue

At the seaside

sun hat

air bed

deck chair

swimmer

beach ball

ice cream

windbreak

pebbles

sun

snorkel

flippers

starfish

suntan lotion

rubber ring

trunks

spade

bucket

swimming costume

sailing boat

lighthouse

radio

surfer

net

bikini

buoy

seagull

cave

seashell

rock

wave

telescope

crab

rockpool

sunglasses

sandcastle

sailboard

speedboat

beach

seaweed

dinghy

43

Weather words

clouds

flood

wind

**MONTHS
OF THE
YEAR**

January

February

March

April

May

June

July

August

September

October

November

December

WINDY

STORMY

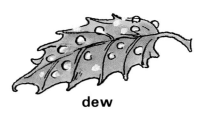
dew

fog

snowman

frost

rainbow

mist

gale

snowball

SUNNY

sun

snow

thunder and lightning

whirlwind

puddle

SNOWY

breeze

ice

rain

storm

45

Things we do

catch

throw

jump

sneeze

drink

ski

skip

swim

eat

sing

sleep

clap

push

write

wave

laugh

run

paint

sit

climb

read

stand

pull

trip

buy

cry

wash

walk

sew

dry

play

dig

dance

watch

listen

cut

dress

yawn

sweep

frown

lick

stick

People

mountaineer

artist

butcher

American footballer

dustman

weight-lifter

typist

decorator

athlete

dentist

taxi driver

carpenter

chef

tennis player

diver

astronaut

skier

hairdresser

jockey

postman

skater

miner

waiter

singer

firefighter

optician

scientist

doctor

baker

lumberjack

policeman

gymnast

computer programmer

49

Opposite words

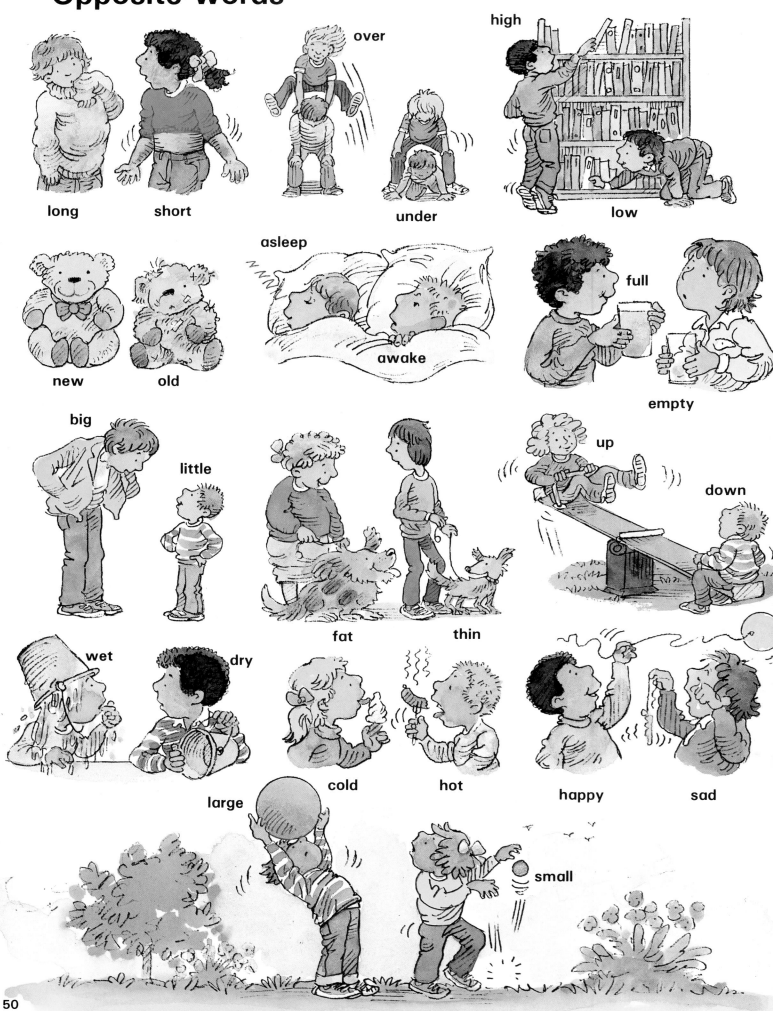

long short

over

under

high

low

new old

asleep

awake

full

empty

big

little

fat thin

up

down

wet dry

cold hot

happy sad

large

small

My week

Monday

I bought a toy plane.

Tuesday

I went to my friend's house to fly my plane.

Wednesday

After school, I flew my plane again. It flew well.

Thursday

I went to Grandma's house. My plane came down with a crash.

Friday

I couldn't fly my plane.

Saturday

Today Mum mended my plane.

Sunday

My plane crashed again. I think I'll buy a bigger, stronger one next week... or perhaps a rocket.

What time is it?

1 — **seven o'clock** — "It's time to get up"

2 — **quarter to eight** — Breakfast time

4 — **quarter past ten** — "Those look nice!"

5 — **twelve o'clock** — "Lunch time. I'm hungry!"

8 — **five o'clock** — "What's for supper?"

9 — **quarter past seven** — Bath time

Colours and shapes

Find these colours in the picture...

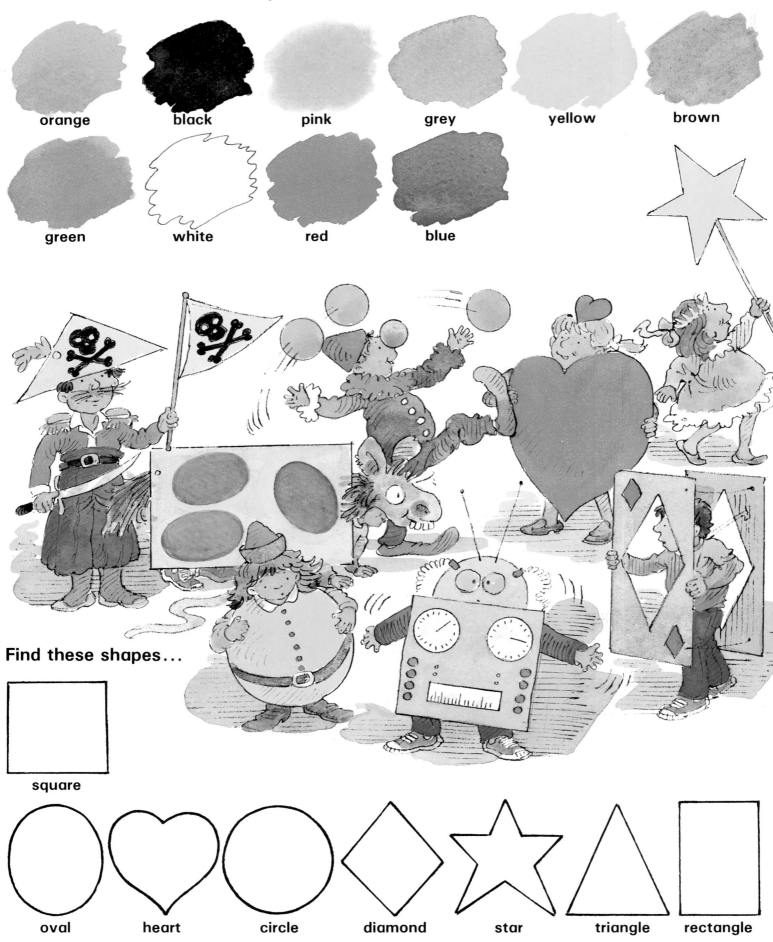

orange black pink grey yellow brown

green white red blue

Find these shapes...

square

oval heart circle diamond star triangle rectangle

Numbers

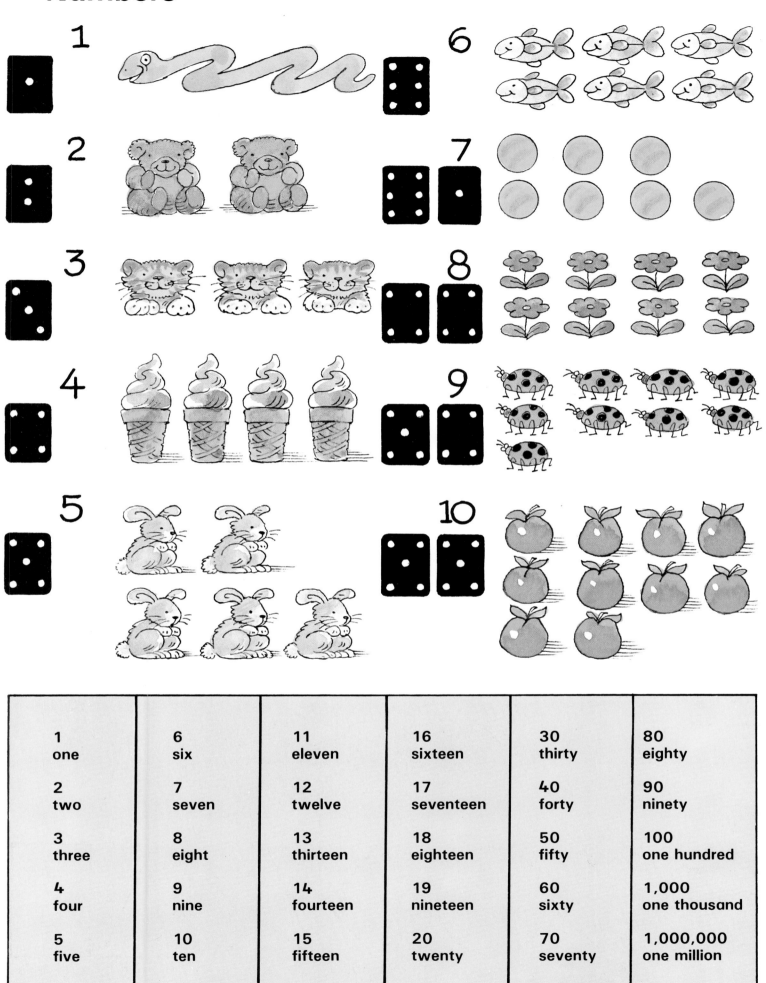

1 one	6 six	11 eleven	16 sixteen	30 thirty	80 eighty
2 two	7 seven	12 twelve	17 seventeen	40 forty	90 ninety
3 three	8 eight	13 thirteen	18 eighteen	50 fifty	100 one hundred
4 four	9 nine	14 fourteen	19 nineteen	60 sixty	1,000 one thousand
5 five	10 ten	15 fifteen	20 twenty	70 seventy	1,000,000 one million

Index

A

B

C

M

magazine 10
mailbag 26
mallet 41
manhole 15
map 20, 41
March 44
margarine 17
marrow 16
mask 19
mast 29
May 44
me 2
meat 16
mechanic 37
medicine 18
melons 17
milk 16
milk tanker 38
million 55
miner 49
mirror 12, 36
mist 45
mixing bowl 9
Monday 51
monkey 25
months 44
mop 8
mother 4
motorcycle 15
mountaineer 48
mountain 41
mouse 5
mouth 2
mouth wash 19
mug 8
mum 4, 51
mushrooms 17

N

nails 35
nature chart 21
neck 2
nest 41
net 43
new 50
newspaper 10, 23
newsstand 15
nightdress 3
nine 55
nineteen 55

ninety 55
nose 2
November 44
numbers 55
nurse 18

O

oar 29
o'clock 52, 53
October 44
oil can 37
old 50
one 55
onions 17
operating theatre 18
opposite words 50
optician 49
orange 54
oranges 17
ostrich 24
otter 41
oval 54
oven 9
over 50

P

paddling pool 22
paint 46
paints 21
panda 24
pants 3
paper 20
parcel 33
park 22-23, 53
parrot 4, 25
passengers 26
pavement 15
pears 17
pebbles 42
pedal bin 9
pelican 25
pencils 20
penguin 25
pens 20
people 48-49
pepper 11
perch 5
petrol pump 15, 36
pets 4-5
pick 35
picnic 22

picture 10
pig 39
pigsty 39
pillow 13
pilot 30
pineapple 17
pink 54
plane 51
plant 11, 18
plaster cast 18
plate 8, 11
platform 27
play 47
pliers 36
plough 38
plumber 34
polar bear 24
policeman 14, 49
pond 39
porthole 28
postcards 33
poster 12
postman 49
potatoes 17
puddle 45
pull 46
puppy 5
push 46
pushchair 23
pyjamas 3, 13

Q

quarter past 52
quarter to 52, 53
quay 28
queue 32
quilt 12

R

rabbit 5, 41
raccoon 24
radar 31
radiator 10
radio 10, 43
railings 22
railway station 26-27
rain 45
rainbow 45
raincoat 3
rainhat 3
rake 7

read 46
records 10
rectangle 54
red 54
refrigerator 9
rhinoceros 25
ribbon 22
river 40
rock 43
rocket 51
rockpool 43
roller skates 22
rolling pin 9
roof tiles 35
rope 28
rotor blades 30
roundabout 23
rowing boat 29, 40
rubber 21
rubber duck 13
rubber ring 23, 42
rucksack 26, 40
rug 10
ruler 20
run 46
runway 30

S

sack 39
sad 50
saddle 38
sailboard 43
sailing boat 28, 42
salt 11
sandcastle 43
satchel 20
Saturday 51
sauce bottle 11
saucepan 9
saucer 8
sausages 17
saw 34
scaffolding 35
scales 12, 21, 29
scarecrow 38
scarf 3
school 51
scientist 49
scissors 20
screen 19
seagull 28, 43
seal 25
seashell 43
seaside 42-43
seat belt 36
seaweed 43

seesaw 23
September 44
settee 10
seven 55
seventeen 55
seventy 55
sew 47
shampoo 12
shapes 54
shaver 12
sheep 38
sheepdog 39
ship 28
shirt 3
shoes 3
shopping 14
shopping bag 14, 33
short 50
shorts 3
shoulder 2
shovel 34
shower 13
sickle 39
sideboard 11
sieve 9
signal 26
signpost 41
silo 38
sing 46
singer 49
sink 8
sister 4
sit 46
six 55
sixteen 55
sixty 55
skater 49
ski 46
skier 41, 49
skip 46
skipping rope 23
skirt 3
sleep 46
slide 22
sling 18
slippers 12, 19
small 50
snack bar 33
snail 6
snake 25
sneeze 46
snorkel 42
snow 45
snowball 45
snowman 44
snowy 45
soap 13
socks 3

son 4
spade 7, 42
spanner 36
speaker 10
speedboat 43
sponge 13
spoon 9, 11
square 54
squirrel 41
stable 4, 38
stand 46
star 54
starfish 42
steering wheel 37
steps 30
stethoscope 18
stick 47
stomach 2
stool 8
storm 45
stormy 44
story 53
straw bales 39
street 14-15
sugar 17
suitcase 27, 31
sun 42, 45
Sunday 51
sunglasses 43
sun hat 42
sunny 45
suntan lotion 42
supermarket 16-17
supper 52
surfer 43
sweater 3
sweep 47
sweet corn 17
swim 46
swimmer 42
swimming costume 22, 42
swings 23
syringe 18

T

table 10
table mat 11
tablecloth 11
tail 30
talcum powder 13
tank 5
tanker 28, 30, 38
tap(s) 8, 13
tape 10